Teaching Little Fingers to Play More Disney Tunes

Piano Solos with Optional Teacher Accompaniments
Arranged by
Glenda Austin

CONTENTS

Disney characters and artwork © Disney Enterprises, Inc.

ISBN 978-1-4234-3124-4

WILLIS MUSIC

T0057329

EXCLUSIVELY DISTRIBUTED BY

7777 W. BLUEMOUND RD. P.O. BOX 13819 MILWAUKEE, WI 53213

Visit Hal Leonard Online at
www.halleonard.com

Circle of Life

from Walt Disney Pictures' THE LION KING

Optional Teacher Accompaniment

Music by Elton John
Lyrics by Tim Rice
Arr. Glenda Austin

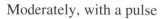

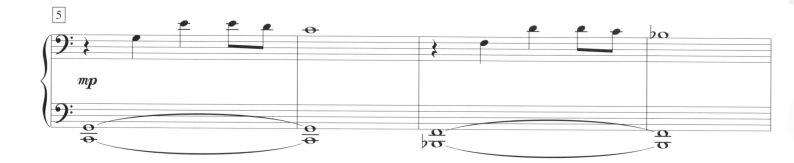

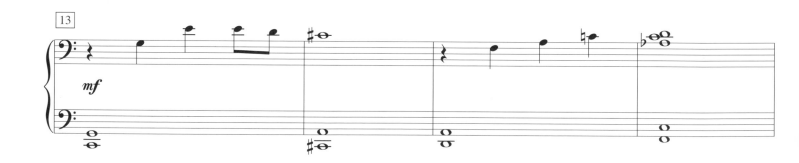

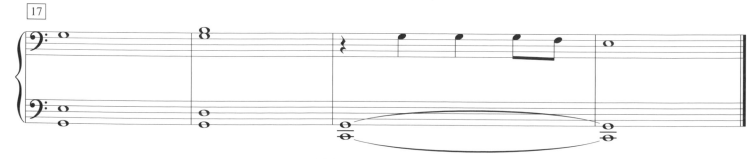

Circle of Life
from Walt Disney Pictures' THE LION KING

Music by Elton John
Lyrics by Tim Rice
Arr. Glenda Austin

Play both hands one octave higher when performing as a duet.

Moderately, with a pulse

A Spoonful of Sugar

from Walt Disney's MARY POPPINS

Optional Teacher Accompaniment

Words and Music by Richard M. Sherman
and Robert B. Sherman
Arr. Glenda Austin

Cheerfully

A Spoonful of Sugar

from Walt Disney's MARY POPPINS

Words and Music by Richard M. Sherman
and Robert B. Sherman
Arr. Glenda Austin

Play both hands one octave higher when performing as a duet.

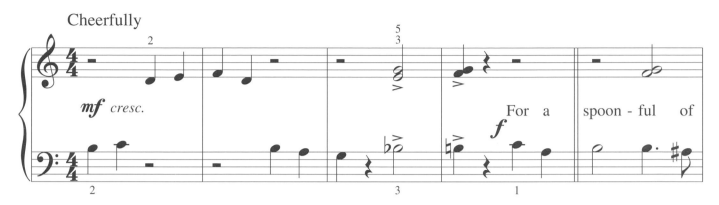

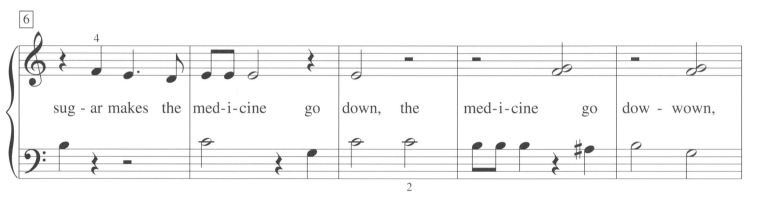

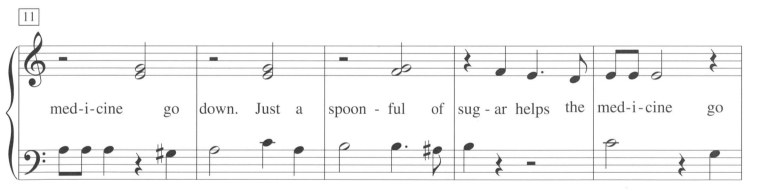

Go the Distance

from Walt Disney Pictures' HERCULES

Optional Teacher Accompaniment

Music by Alan Menken
Lyrics by David Zippel
Arr. Glenda Austin

With longing

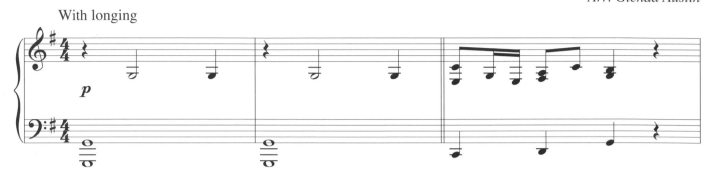

Go the Distance
from Walt Disney Pictures' HERCULES

Music by Alan Menken
Lyrics by David Zippel
Arr. Glenda Austin

Play both hands one octave higher when performing as a duet.

Optional Teacher Accompaniment

there some-day,   I can go the dis-tance. I will   find   my   way

if   I   can   be strong.   I know   ev - 'ry   mile   will   be

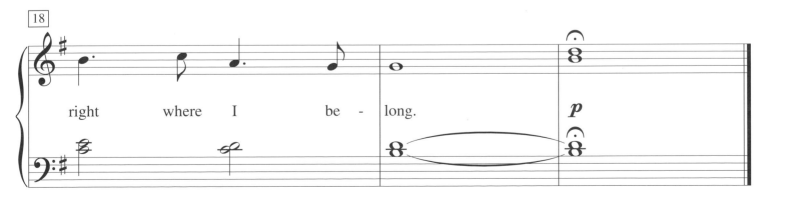

worth   my   while.   When   I   go   the   dis-tance,   I'll   be

right   where   I   be - long.

A Whole New World
from Walt Disney's ALADDIN

Optional Teacher Accompaniment

Music by Alan Menken
Lyrics by Tim Rice
Arr. Glenda Austin

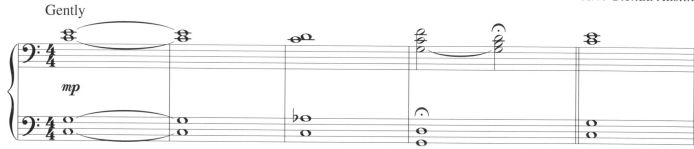

A Whole New World
from Walt Disney's ALADDIN

Music by Alan Menken
Lyrics by Tim Rice
Arr. Glenda Austin

Play both hands one octave higher when performing as a duet.

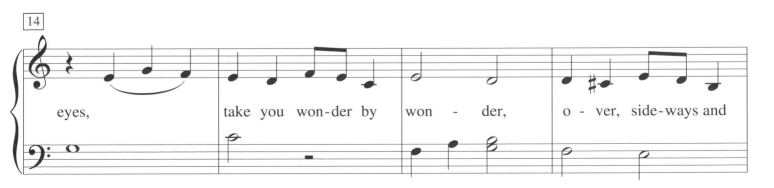

Optional Teacher Accompaniment

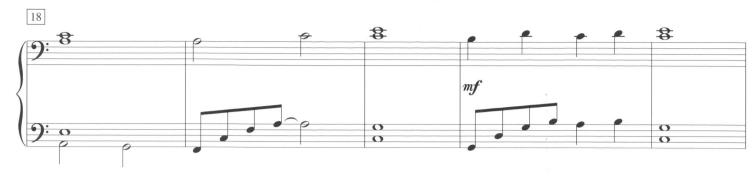

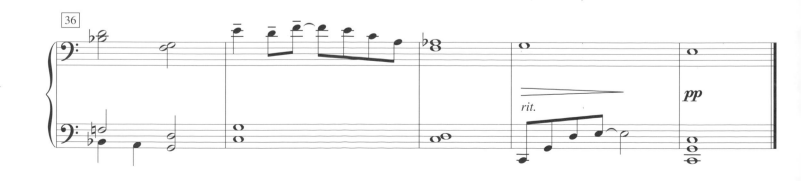

Little April Shower
from Walt Disney's BAMBI

Optional Teacher Accompaniment

Words by Larry Morey
Music by Frank Churchill
Arr. Glenda Austin

With a little bounce

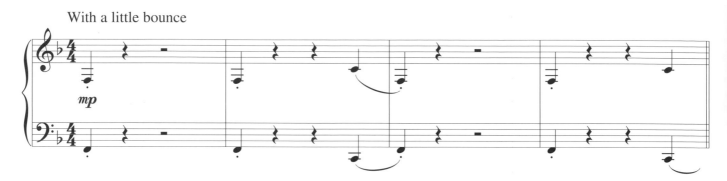

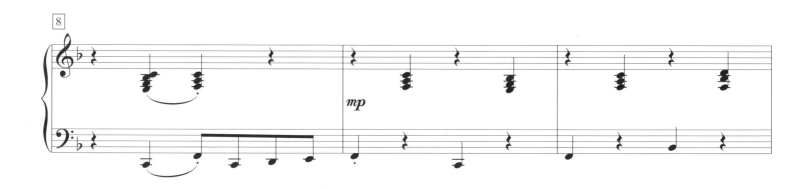

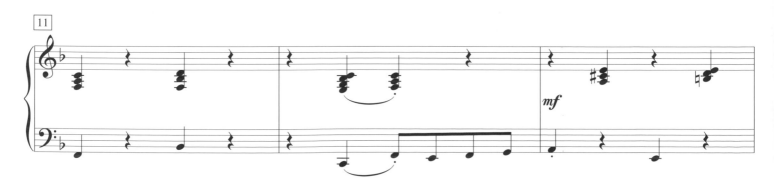

Little April Shower
from Walt Disney's BAMBI

Words by Larry Morey
Music by Frank Churchill
Arr. Glenda Austin

Play both hands one octave higher when performing as a duet.

With a little bounce

Optional Teacher Accompaniment

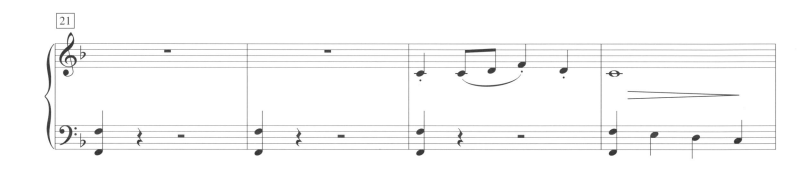

sky is cloud - y, your pret - ty mu - sic can bright - en the day.

Drip, drip, drop, when the sun says "How - dy," you say "Good-bye" right a - way.

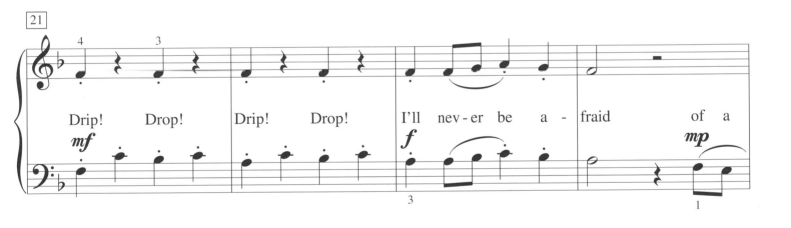

Drip! Drop! Drip! Drop! I'll nev - er be a - fraid of a

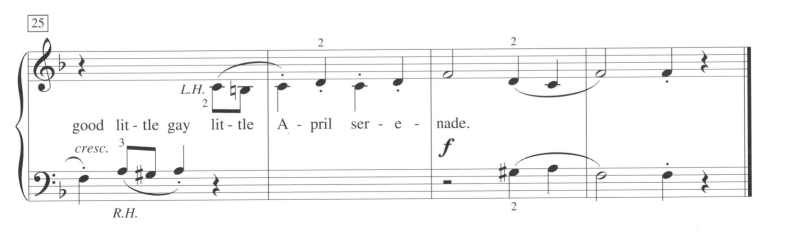

good lit - tle gay lit - tle A - pril ser - e - nade.

Colors of the Wind
from Walt Disney's POCAHONTAS

Optional Teacher Accompaniment

Music by Alan Menken
Lyrics by Stephen Schwartz
Arr. Glenda Austin

Colors of the Wind
from Walt Disney's POCAHONTAS

Music by Alan Menken
Lyrics by Stephen Schwartz
Arr. Glenda Austin

Play both hands one octave higher when performing as a duet.

Optional Teacher Accompaniment

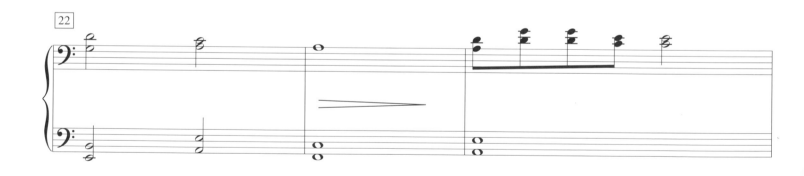

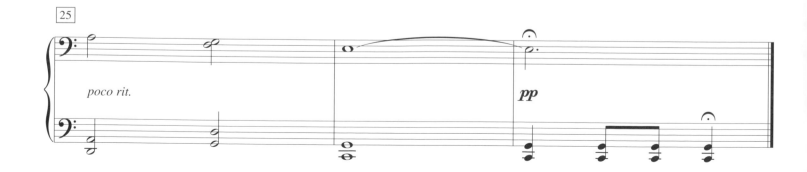

A Dream Is a Wish
Your Heart Makes

from Walt Disney's CINDERELLA

Optional Teacher Accompaniment

Words and Music by Mack David,
Al Hoffman and Jerry Livingston
Arr. Glenda Austin

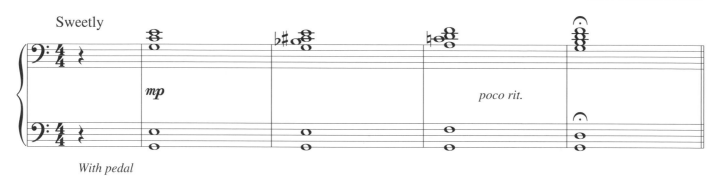

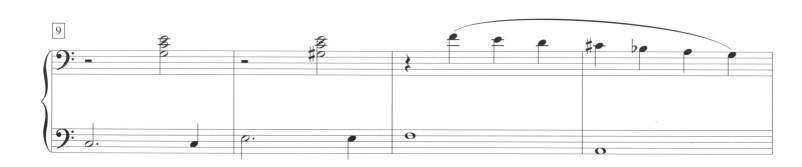

A Dream Is a Wish Your Heart Makes

from Walt Disney's CINDERELLA

Words and Music by Mack David,
Al Hoffman and Jerry Livingston
Arr. Glenda Austin

Play both hands one octave higher when performing as a duet.

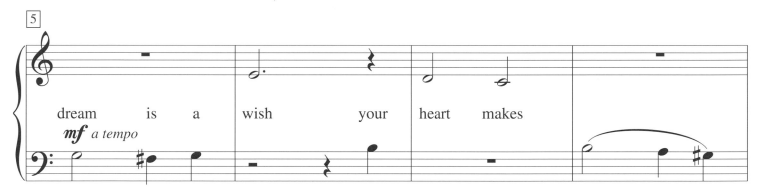

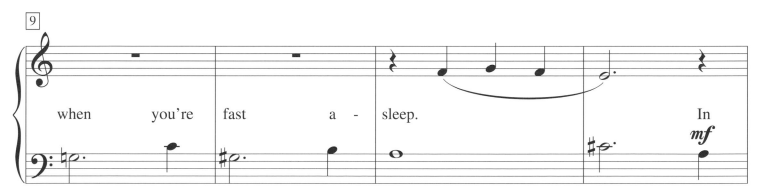

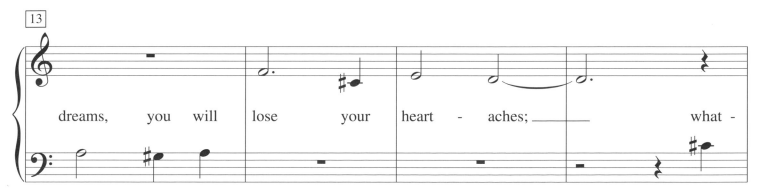

Optional Teacher Accompaniment

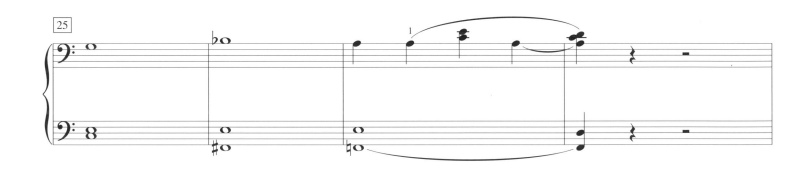

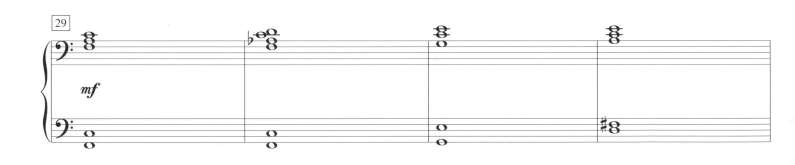

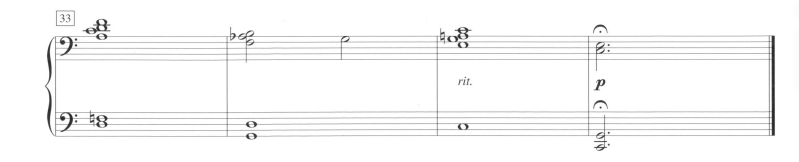

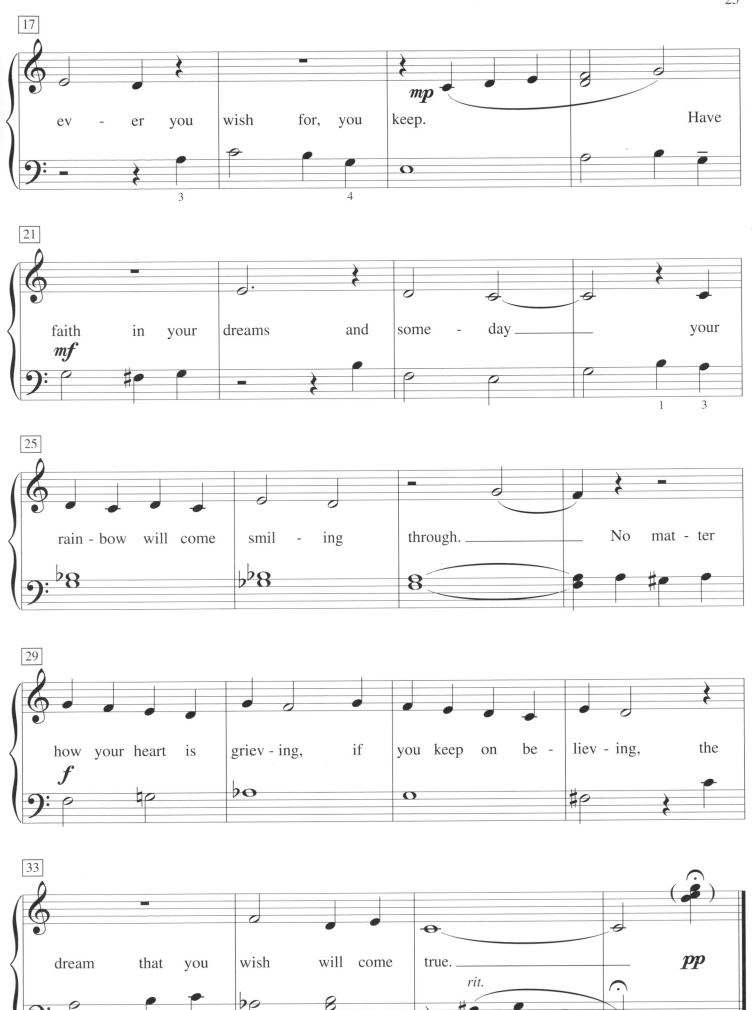

Cruella De Vil

from Walt Disney's 101 DALMATIANS

Optional Teacher Accompaniment

Words and Music by
Mel Leven
Arr. Glenda Austin

Cruella De Vil
from Walt Disney's 101 DALMATIANS

Words and Music by
Mel Leven
Arr. Glenda Austin

Play both hands one octave higher when playing as a duet.

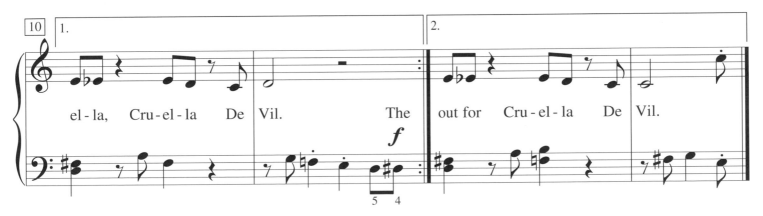

Under the Sea
from Walt Disney's THE LITTLE MERMAID

Optional Teacher Accompaniment

Lyrics by Howard Ashman
Music by Alan Menken
Arr. Glenda Austin

Under the Sea
from Walt Disney's THE LITTLE MERMAID

Lyrics by Howard Ashman
Music by Alan Menken
Arr. Glenda Austin

Play both hands one octave higher when performing as a duet.

With energy

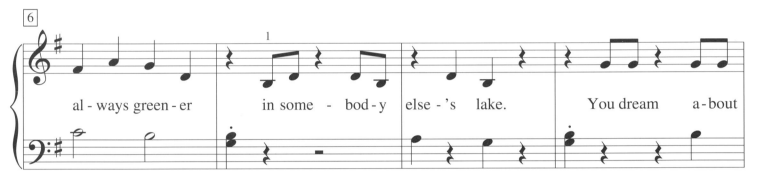

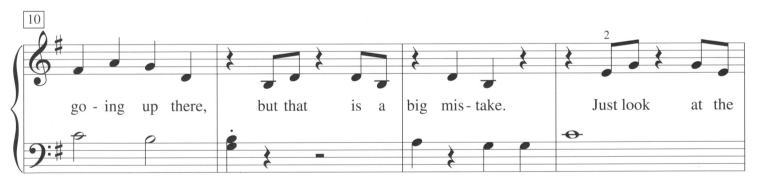

Optional Teacher Accompaniment

things sur-round you. What more is you look-in' for? Un-der the

sea, un-der the sea. Dar-lin', it's bet-ter down where it's

wet-ter. Take it from me. Up on the shore they work all day,

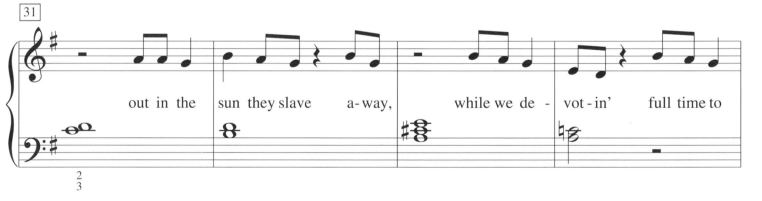

out in the sun they slave a-way, while we de - vot-in' full time to

float-in' un-der the sea.

TEACHING LITTLE FINGERS TO PLAY MORE

TEACHING LITTLE FINGERS TO PLAY MORE
by Leigh Kaplan

Teaching Little Fingers to Play More is a fun-filled and colorfully illustrated follow-up book to *Teachi... Little Fingers to Play*. It strengthens skills learned while carefully easing the transition into John Thompson Modern Course, First Grade.

00406137 Book only $6.99
00406527 Book/Audio $9.99

SUPPLEMENTARY SERIES
All books include optional teacher accompaniments.

BROADWAY SONGS
arr. Carolyn Miller
MID TO LATER ELEMENTARY LEVEL
10 great show tunes for students to enjoy, including: Edelweiss • I Whistle a Happy Tune • I Won't Grow Up • Maybe • The Music of the Night • and more.
00416928 Book only $6.99
00416929 Book/Audio $12.99

CHILDREN'S SONGS
arr. Carolyn Miller
MID-ELEMENTARY LEVEL
10 songs: The Candy Man • Do-Re-Mi • I'm Popeye the Sailor Man • It's a Small World • Linus and Lucy • The Muppet Show Theme • Sesame Street Theme • Supercalifragilisticexpialidocious • Tomorrow.
00416810 Book only $6.99
00416811 Book/Audio $12.99

CLASSICS
arr. Randall Hartsell
MID-ELEMENTARY LEVEL
7 solos: Marche Slave • Over the Waves • Polovtsian Dance (from the opera *Prince Igor*) • Pomp and Circumstance • Rondeau • Waltz (from the ballet *Sleeping Beauty*) • William Tell Overture.
00406760 Book only $5.99
00416513 Book/Audio $10.99

DISNEY TUNES
arr. Glenda Austin
MID-ELEMENTARY LEVEL
9 songs, including: Circle of Life • Colors of the Wind • A Dream Is a Wish Your Heart Makes • A Spoonful of Sugar • Under the Sea • A Whole New World • and more.
00416750 Book only $9.99
00416751 Book/Audio $12.99

EASY DUETS
arr. Carolyn Miller
MID-ELEMENTARY LEVEL
9 equal-level duets: A Bicycle Built for Two • Blow the Man Down • Chopsticks • Do Your Ears Hang Low? • I've Been Working on the Railroad • The Man on the Flying Trapeze • Short'nin' Bread • Skip to My Lou • The Yellow Rose of Texas.
00416832 Book only $6.99
00416833 Book/Audio $10.99

JAZZ AND ROCK
Eric Baumgartner
MID-ELEMENTARY LEVEL
11 solos, including: Big Bass Boogie • Crescendo Rock • Funky Fingers • Jazz Waltz in G • Rockin' Rhythm • Squirrel Race • and more!
00406765 Book only $5.99

MOVIE MUSIC
arr. Carolyn Miller
LATER ELEMENTARY LEVEL
10 magical movie arrangements: Bella's Lullaby (Twilight) • Somewhere Out There (An American Tail) • True Love's Kiss (Enchanted) • and more.
00139190 Book/Audio $10.99

Also available:

AMERICAN TUNES
arr. Eric Baumgartner
MID-ELEMENTARY LEVEL
00406755 Book only $6.99

BLUES AND BOOGIE
Carolyn Miller
MID-ELEMENTARY LEVEL
00406764 Book only $5.99

CHRISTMAS CAROLS
arr. Carolyn Miller
MID-ELEMENTARY LEVEL
00406763 Book only $6.99

CHRISTMAS CLASSICS
arr. Eric Baumgartner
MID-ELEMENTARY LEVEL
00416827 Book only $6.99
00416826 Book/Audio $12.99

CHRISTMAS FAVORITES
arr. Eric Baumgartner
MID-ELEMENTARY LEVEL
00416723 Book only $7.99
00416724 Book/Audio $12.99

FAMILIAR TUNES
arr. Glenda Austin
MID-ELEMENTARY LEVEL
00406761 Book only $6.99

HYMNS
arr. Glenda Austin
MID-ELEMENTARY LEVEL
00406762 Book only $6.99

JEWISH FAVORITES
arr. Eric Baumgartner
MID-ELEMENTARY LEVEL
00416755 Book only $5.99

RECITAL PIECES
Carolyn Miller
MID-ELEMENTARY LEVEL
00416540 Book only $5.99

SONGS FROM MANY LAND...
arr. Carolyn C. Setliff
MID-ELEMENTARY LEVEL
00416688 Book only $5.99

EXCLUSIVELY DISTRIBUTED BY

Hal•Leonard®

Complete song lists online at
www.halleonard.com